TRIAL OF THE SENSES

THE HEART OF A POET

ALPHABET CLUB

Dedicated to love , whatever that is.

Contents

Contents

Preface

In this masterclass in effervescent wordcraft, even as it ranges through troubled terrain, Alphabet Club proves to be a conglomerate of poets with the love of sanity. The book is a mirror; the deeper you delve, the more clearly it reflects your own life's path.

Acknowledgements

This time, we'd like to thank all of you for sticking with us through this roller coaster of a saga, through cliff hangers and angst and feels. We'd never trade you for anything. All of the authors of the first issue anthology send their love and appreciation to you.

The unwavering support of Parul University, India, and all of its departments has been invaluable in this project. With everything laid out for Alphabet Club to produce poetry issues on a monthly basis. More is in store for our readers. Stay tuned!

1. Dear Depression

Is it not yet time to have enough of me?
Are you not satisfied with everything or you just can't see?
You clearly see the damages and decide not to leave?
I'm not okay with you, why don't you believe?
I wish I can kick you out but I'm tired
Tired of you aching my head and making my brain wired
Just find a different host and reside
My life is falling apart, would you mind if I decide?
Yes, for our own good and trust me it's going to be fair
More than enough to settle everything between us
With negotiations you can peacefully leave with no fare
Just leave and let me because it really sucks
This attitude nearly killed me and caused me migraine
A deadly attitude that has no inch to invade in my brain.

Isaac Amo Essien
Ghana

2. When I'm Gone

They all know that you'll miss me more
You'd realize I was the only one you had to adore
Who'd be around to show you real love?
I'll be forever gone, let me be the best you'll ever have
Let me be your first and not your second
I'm not convincing you to make me your best
Romeo died because of love, such a legend
Dying because of love is not something I'd not want to test
But if it happens don't bring me flowers
Sit by me while I sadly rest for hours
You'd be left alone crying but only for a year
I won't be appearing in your dreams because you wouldn't
Be expecting me there
Love me now and make me your number one
So that we both wake up to see the rising sun.
Isaac Amo Essien
Ghana

3. Where did she go?

The softest hands ever held
Grandma's name is beauty
Neither alive nor dead
She spoke many emotions
A sea of emotions covered her eyes
The day she asked me to pray
I was into pieces
"Just today", all I asked.
But another day meant more pain
Her body getting smaller
My fist covered all of her feet.
7 spoons of water
Was the act of love
and acceptance of the possibility.
She laid with tears,
Ready to go wherever her years spend.
She said, "I now see that it used to be difficult."
That was the last of her.
Baiahun Talang
India

4. A foreign land

• 4 •

In a foreign land,
I took off the old rag.
Putting on life,
A new heart
I take home.
Baiahun Talang
India

5. Gentleman's Touch

At ease I was

His soft warm fingers ran through my shoulder

Are you hurt?

Tell me!

I'm perfectly fine she whispered softly and swiftly

The gaze into her eyes made her twinkle

The tone of his voice made her melt

Who he was no one knew

He greeted me once but it left a mark

An emptiness that needed more of his soothing voice

His strides long and brief his smile genuine but inciting

His lips thin and tight

He touched me, rubbed me and felt me as l trembled under
his simple touch

I was in flames filled with pain of the way I wanted more from
a stranger who was now

Danger which was about temper with my inner demons

The Gentlemen

Rugare Elgivva Takunda Jani

Zimbabwe

6. All was vanity

Just like politics, Its a gamble
A game of thrones. A war
It's so infuriating, Yet so enticing
Imagine a place where you get to
Wine and dine with the devil
Betrayal
Dismantled and shattered into pieces
It was high time
To erase the four words
And just let it pump blood
Don't get it twisted
Love is a beautiful thing
He made me feel heaven on earth
But my board did not have a stales or check mate
Rugare Elgivva Takunda Jani
Zimbabwe

7. Will you?

You are the package I received,
It's true that the address is mine,
I got you in the right time and that's fine.
But the question is,
Will you?
Stay,
Be mine forever,
Be the same package.
Or can I conclude,
Will you?
Leave without a goodbye,
Leave me with a lot of questions.
Can I hear from you?
Or will you?
Give me the answer,
Or will you?
Not answer at the moment.

Angel Nanyaro

Tanzania

8. Till the sun gets cold

How do you see the sun?
It's so shinning right,
So beautiful and bright,
Absolutely.
How do you feel its warmth?
It's so hot and burns constantly,
No matter what it still shines,
So independent,
Exactly.
Babe take a look at it,
Hold my breath and hear this,
I love you till the sun gets cold.
Angel Nanyaro
Tanzania

9. The illusion of the heart

• 9 •

Love, trust, forever those are just,
Images of the heart they do not exist,
You seemed so perfect to be the one,
But alas I was dreaming!
I thought for once I had joined the correct,
Road but alas I was lost. So many dreams,
And hopes that if I remanence it breaks my heart,
Seemed to have been the one but alas, you made,
Me know pain only.
Wastage of love, time gone and lost.
Heartbreak l fear but now has appeared.
I thought for once the stars had remembered,
Me but l was just a fool was not thinking,
I had blindly trusted now hatred builds up.
Charity Runganga
Zimbabwe

10. Hear the plight of an opharn

I am innocent, done evil to non,
I don't know the use of weapons,
Nor to curse why oh why must they.
Be tears on my eyes why do other rejoice
Kids yet I suffer!
I am only subjected to mourning and.
Overthinking, oh my lord you are not dead
Hear my cry my prayers for I wish to
Experience the laughter other children do.
Hear my plight, hear my cry for I wish to
Belong to the happy home.
Charity Runganga
Zimbabwe

11. My Once Upon

You used to be my once upon
A dream now you like my once
Upon a scream!
Roses, kisses, forever I imagined,
But alas my mind had been lost!
Realization of what we had shared been gone
Escalated in my heart aching and shivering
But that was the way to live with peace...
The soothening words I used to remanence on
Suddenly vanished into the quick mist were
Only the fog can tell the story.
Deep deep inside my chambers vessels
Broke into trillion pieces which were never
To be mended not compelled the love had
Died!
Charity Runganga
Zimbabwe

12. A Student

Student life is the best
Student life is the greatest
And student life forever remains in our
Lives as one of the memorable and
Precious thing we have ever
Experienced
Therefore it is up to you to decide today
How you want these years as a student to
Be
It is up to you today to decide what kind of
life you will live
what kind of grades you will get
what kind of relationships you will create
what kind of sports you will involve
yourself with
what kind of marks you will leave after
your program at this university
Only today itself the very beginning of
Student life that's the day you have to decide
For this is where you will learn the value of
hard work
value of love and life
value of sacrifice

different cultures
different beliefs
And different experience.
But one thing you should know also Is that
This path of student life is not easy also
You will meet people who will compete with you
People who will look down on you
People who won't notice your presence
But listen you are not here to compete
With anyone but yourself
Moreover you are here to achieve your
Goals
To work hard
Studies develop brain power
Thanks
Samahan Namonje
Zambia

13. What is Success?

Success is overcoming the fear to
fail.
Success is turning that which is
impossible to possibility..
Success is trying despite the challenge
you face while trying...
Above all things Success start from your
mind.
As they say you are who you think...
It's not easy to be successful,,
Success is the road full of rivers and
mountains
If you want to make it you have to cross
rivers, crib mountains and be thirsty...
Rivers those are challenges which will
come around you
Samahan Namonje
Zambia

14. Brown skin girl

Oh brown skin girl,
what a beauty you are...
see how you shine like a Star
your hair is so beautiful and adorable
your colour shines even in the darkness
look at your eyes,
oh queen of beauty.
They say you are not beutiful,
they call you black,
they say your hair is like of the mop,
they say your eyes are very dark.
They call you all kinds of names
some see you as a sex tool,
Some say you don't deserve better,
some tell you to lighten your skin,
some tell you to cover your hair with
other hair
Oh brown skin girl don't listen to what
they say..
you are enough,
you are deserving,
you are intelligent,
you are beautiful,

see how pretty you are...
you are like a brown chocolate,
don't change your skin for anyone,
don't obey when they put pain on you,
don't let their talk enter into your sweet
heart,
if you do their words can build up in you
you are beautiful,
see how pretty you are...
you are like a brown chocolate,
don't change your skin for anyone,
don't obey when they put pain on you,
don't let their talk enter into your sweet
heart,
if you do their words can build up in you
you are beautiful,
see how pretty you are...
you are like a brown chocolate,
don't change your skin for anyone,
don't obey when they put pain on you,
don't let their talk enter into your sweet
heart,
if you do their words can build up in you
and block you from seeing how
wonderful you are.
Oh brown skin girl listen to your heart
your colour is so expensive,

your colour can't be bought,

remember you are beautiful.

yes you are don't doubt it...

Samahan Namonje

Zambia

15. Man in the Mirror

Blurred by the color of her shinning black brown eyes Yet still,
Her smile bragging to the mirror on how pretty it is
Her lips moving left, right and center proud of the goddess
they have become
But the question remains-
Who is the man in the Mirror?
Idolizing her complexion
Proud of the way the sun seems to be kissing it all day
Her body still bragging on how the outfit shapes her
silhouette
"Looking Peng" words of worship in her ears
Smiles of pleasure fill her inner soul
But the question remains-
Who is the man in the mirror?
Matipaishe Mavunga
Zimbabwe

16. Ghost

Just like leaves falling from a tree

Turn my soul into a ghost.

Make my being vanish;

For the deeds of this world overburden my strengths.

Just like sea waves leaving the seashore

Turn me into a ghost.

Make my memory erased;

For who l am is what l fail to give an answer to.

Just like a Father accepting His prodigal son.

Embrace me into your arms;

For that's where l only feel safe Take your mud and mold me

once more-

Matipaishe Mavunga

Zimbabwe

17. Dear Diary:- Part 1

There is a big black hole in my heart
Where you used to be
I tell people that i moved on
I can see that you already did
And i too tried to move
And i did move
But the memories stayed still
Sometimes i go back to the time we
were together
Regretting saying hi to you the first time
Regretting having all those great moments with you
Because those moments have lead me
to my sorrow and sadness
This black hole sucks away all the
happy things i try too feel
It snatches the warmth that i once
used to have
Because whatever I do
now I always feel incomplete.
PS:- it's about friends
Surabi Sharma
India

18. Cycle

The cycle of trusting someone and getting
your heart shattered never ends
The feeling of ripping your veins open never
goes away
You smile and laugh and sing
But your heart is frowning and crying and
sobbing
Surabi Sharma
India

19. The Love Driver

Wishful bricks of breathable moments
The moments that caught up
The moments that weren't sure to exist
And then just happened
The moments of you and I.
Hallucinating the warmth
Of a life that I never lived
And then you made sure to not let those go
The brief earthy smiles that I heaved.
You stayed, of course you did.
Did you ever notice the sky turning grey
I never could for I feared the grave disappointment, of not
finding one
Then you had a sweater with the silver lining
And the cold hit
I remember, you rolled up the sleeves, called me stupid.
I never lived through the emotion flowers, and I forget they
named it love
But the interrogations embarked at the end of a star studded
sky
Did you just let me go, or did I just gave it up, could never be
enough.
Even the shrieky loneliness couldn't fill up the heavy silences

Can I scream out loud for you to fix the imbalances
You always did.
The proximity is tiresome and amusing
You crept up on me just as did the scent of your pullover
How do I fathom the insanity of the blame so consumed
For it was the precarious, yet comforting love driver.
Janvee Singh
India

20. Unconventional

The faded skies
Had a hue so dark
A jaunty ride
For one to embark
Grinning wide
Yet a breaking clout
Screeching silence
But you never shout.
Consumed by the orb
Scrutiny of the living
Being yourself
Or what away one is giving.
Bags so dark
Looks pale they say
Dorns the rainbow
But lives so grey.
Spilling the ink
Modus operandi crafted
Leaning on the hence
A present was drafted.
Sui generis as one shined
Bracing the peculiarities
Unconventional one might be

For individuals have individualities

Janvee Singh

India

21. Daisy-My Lovely Flower

Finally, I have found you.
Vibrant as the sun,
by a single gaze, you enchant me.
For,
I am your bee,
attracted to your sweet nectar,
I chase you like a shadow.
Drunk from your sugary delight,
I buzz a song,
that only your heart recognizes.
Cheerful in the wind,
you dance.
In between the rocks,
where you chose to conceal your beauty.
How,I wish to see the world,
salivate over your entice.
By my small wings,
I carry you to the Heavens.
And in the clouds,
we take a moment to hide.
On your yellow center,
To feel the color and texture,

Till eternity,
forever l reside.
Kelvin Saungweme
Zimbabwe

22. Just Friends

Once upon a time,
the rivers of my heart were blocked.
I stood only a breath away from you,
drowning in conversations we can't begin to utter.
Although close, you were far away.
Although present, you were absent.
With this burning sensation in my heart,
A wildfire, I couldn't ever tame.
For I was trapped in a reverie,
A dream of what we could be,
The warmth of a kiss that we could have.
For this tantalizing love,
to finally grow roots,
A question finally escaped my lips.
Do you love me? I asked.
In your silence,
you just stood there.
In your hesitation, I knew.
Kelvin Saungweme
Zimbabwe

23. Immmaculation

Is it your exquisite shoulders at par with the wings of alluring angels?

Or is it the way the sun fell in love with you that the heavens seem to have fallen down to earth?

It's the way your eyes shine like golden coins dropped in heaven's drains that makes even the shimmering glitters of the stars that bind the heavens' celestial candles ablaze seem like darkness.

Your face speaks beauty on its own like a cinnamon-coated soliloquy accentuating the edges of your lips like piano keys crafted by the most graceful of angels,

So that every time mine greet yours an instant melody is birthed that plays the strings of my heart's arteries till the skies are gleaming white as the angels shine their smiles upon the earth like David plucked the strings on his harp a second time,

And I just happen to be the pen that writes these enchanting decibels to you.

And when you gaze back at me it's like your eyeballs plead on behalf of your lungs to take a deep breath, because the next time I look at you, you might not breathe again,

Well, both of us might not,

Because our relationship is like that of the ocean and a drowning swimmer, you constantly spike me with the waves

of your body while I try to glide to the surface losing breath with every tide I try to harness with my palms,
These great and magnificent tides on your body that bend like brackets bracketing every synonym of perfection between all your edges and curves are metaphors of what it means to be a work of divine architecture to say the least.
Vinlaw Mudehwe
Zimbabwe

24. Fireflies

• 31 •

I like the way your eyes spontaneously dance in their sockets when mine patiently stay still while piercing into yours like jars stealthy trying to capture brightly excited fireflies in your pupil.

Vinlaw Mudehwe
Zimbabwe

25. This is Me

I would cry
So I can die
Swollen red eye
So I can say goodbye
I had to detoxify myself
To dignify myself
I kept busy by the bookshelf
Till I found self recognition
I have ambition
With no condition
I have done no omission
I know my true definition
Elizabeth Chinguno
Zimbabwe

26. Come back to Earth

You are missed
Come back to earth
You are remembered
Come back to earth
We are left with flesh
To turn to ash,
Not as fresh as before,
Gone with a flash
You are needed
Come back to earth
You are wanted
Come back to earth
We feel your everlasting soul
But can't control
As you patrol the house
Like a lost troll.
Elizabeth Chinguno
Zimbabwe

27. Social Media Standard

Me choosing to live a **SOCIAL MEDIA** standard life

It is early in the morning

Quickly searching for my phone

I have no idea if all of my limbs are present

I have no idea if they are working

Looking at my phone even before talking to my creator

I am busy searching for current news

I am busy looking at the **SOCIAL MEDIA** stars

I am looking of how I need to live today

I am busy looking for how my body shape and size needs to be today

I am looking for current **TRENDING** artificial nails

I am looking for trending shoes

I am looking for trending clothes

I am looking for trending strip lashes (artificial eye lashes)

I need do be the **SOCIAL MEDIA STANDARD**

I can not live any other life

I need to live according to the **SOCIAL MEDIA**

The **SOCIAL MEDIA DEFINITION OF BEUTY IS MY DEFITION**

I am in the world that recognizes beauty in that aspect

I believe that's how I must live my life

When I look at the stars they are my Idol

The world is just perfect if everyone lived and perceived things like social media does.

Its noon already I am surprised

I have had nothing to eat I need to remain in shape

I have not gone outside of the house I wonder how is the weather

Oh! I have not talked to my parents and siblings to know how they are doing

My mother called to check on me I told her I was busy

It is noon I discover I have to do my hair, nails and put other lashes per trends

I haven't had time to talk to my creator I haven't had time to read my books

I haven't had time to talk to myself, I am busy on **SOCIAL MEDIA** need to post my pictures!!

Evergrace Aligawesa
Tanzania

28. A Women Wonder

She is a woman and a mother
She is a superwoman
She is a strong woman
She is a valuable woman
She is an understanding woman
She is a self-empowered woman
She is a responsible woman
With confidence she stands
In enormous ways she understands
In a meticulous way she represents her community
Forward willingly moving
A family, community, country and continent to represent
In various ways she is a supper a great woman
She is a core to her family
She stabilizes a family
She is a multiplier in the family
She brings family together
She is an essence of a stable family
She is a mother to her own siblings and children
She is daily on duty to her family, parents and in-laws
She is full time care giver in the society without payment
Her presence is in a society always notifiable results
Yes Yes Yes she has a golden heart

Yes Yes she has a special place in the society
She is a super woman, she will do anything for her family, she
has a sacrificial heart.

Evergrace Aligawesa
Tanzania

29. Wicked World

They lied - they lied to me,
Had l know, l would have reserved my energy,
Instead, l abused my innocent biceps for invisible gain,
I needlessly trained my body for pain, much to immunity,
I missed hangouts with the boys,
All in name of discipline.
Little did l know l was entertaining false hope.
My bones within me regret and blame me.
They suffered anguish for no reason.
My heart crys in pain.
What is it l skipped?
Burning mid-night coils?
As if l did not starve my eyes their deserving sleep.
I tried every avenue possible,
And loyal to my aggression, humbled all their examinations.
My hope was fueled,
And a rosey future was on horizon,
Within just a few Degrees from reach.
In excitement, l reincarnate my old workaholic self,
The consumer of knowledge atoms.
And as always, the ground responded promisingly.
Surely what could deny the mansion in my dreams.
How l wish I had let them just be dreams,

Because today they've turned into objects of insult to my ambitious self.

I wish had been in touch with reality then.

Maybe l would have been someone today.

Maybe my dreams were too far fetched, perhaps a mentor could have helped,

And now l beg like the man l once felt for

How upset life can be!

If only they taught me the language of relevance.

I could have aligned my skills accordingly.

Maybe l could have read all that was in their library.

In times of disaster l could have stood as their hero

Yet in my cowardice, l exempted my self in guise of study.

While I let my dependents suffer, l did not know they were trusting in my knowledge.

And now l suffer the consequences,

Forever blaming myself for orchestrating my own demise.

Had l know, l would have applied my knowledge.

This I'll sing in the comfort of my oblivion.

David Nemaungwe

Zimbabwe

9798888830840